# National Aboriginal Day

## Heather C. Hudak

Weigl

Published by Weigl Educational Publishers Limited
6325 10 Street S.E.
Calgary, Alberta
T2H 2Z9

www.weigl.com

Library and Archives Canada Cataloguing in Publication data available upon request.
Fax 403-233-7769 for the attention of the Publishing Records department.

ISBN 978-1-55388-521-4 (hard cover)
ISBN 978-1-55388-526-9 (soft cover)

Printed in the United States of America
1 2 3 4 5 6 7 8 9 0  13 12 11 10 09

Editor: Heather C. Hudak
Design: Terry Paulhus

Every reasonable effort has been made to trace ownership and to obtain permission to reprint copyright material. The publishers would be pleased to have any errors or omissions brought to their attention so that they may be corrected in subsequent printings.

Weigl acknowledges Getty Images as one of its primary image suppliers for this title.
Alamy: pages 7, 9, 15, 19; Newscom: page 21.

We gratefully acknowledge the financial support of the Government of Canada through the Book Publishing Industry Development Program (BPIDP) for our publishing activities.

# Contents

# What is National Aboriginal Day?

First Nations, Inuit, and Métis are Canada's Aboriginal Peoples. There is a special day set aside each year to celebrate the **heritage** of these people. It is on June 21 and is known as National Aboriginal Day.

4

# Canada's First People

Aboriginal Peoples were the first people to live in Canada. Each group has its own way of life, language, beliefs, and laws.

# Shaping Canada

Today, there are about one million Aboriginal Peoples in Canada. Their traditions and customs have helped shape the country. National Aboriginal Day is a time for all Canadians to learn more about Aboriginal Peoples' contributions to Canada.

# First Day of Summer

Aboriginal Peoples have celebrated their heritage on or near June 21 for generations. This is the first day of summer. It also is the longest day of the year.

# Celebrating the Season

To celebrate the beginning of summer, Aboriginal Peoples honour nature's beauty. They pay tribute to the fact that the snow is gone and flowers are in bloom.

13

# Recognizing Aboriginal Peoples

A group called the National Indian Brotherhood wanted a special day for all Canadians to honour Aboriginal Peoples. This group first asked the Canadian **government** to declare a holiday in 1982.

# Quebec Declares a Holiday

Quebec's government was the first to recognize Aboriginal Peoples with a special day. In 1990, this province declared that June 21 would be a day to celebrate the ways of Aboriginal Peoples.

# A Day to Celebrate

Then, in 1996, the Government of Canada named June 21 National Aboriginal Day. This is a time for Aboriginal Peoples to share their customs and traditions at special events across Canada. The Hoop Dance is often performed at Aboriginal celebrations.

# Games, Songs, and Dances

People celebrate National Aboriginal Day in many ways. Some play traditional games, such as **lacrosse**. Aboriginal singers and dancers may put on special shows. This often includes drumming.

# Traditional Foods

People eat traditional foods on National Aboriginal Day. **Squash**, beans, corn, and berries are common foods. Bannock is a type of traditional bread. Wild rice is a part of many meals.

# Glossary

# Index

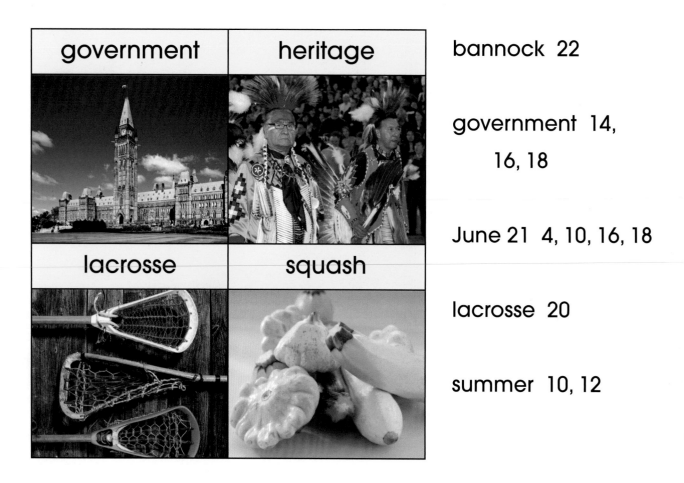

| government | heritage |
|---|---|
| lacrosse | squash |